Original title:
The Truth About Life's Meaning (Spoiler: I Don't Know)

Copyright © 2025 Creative Arts Management OÜ
All rights reserved.

Author: Juliette Kensington
ISBN HARDBACK: 978-1-80566-117-7
ISBN PAPERBACK: 978-1-80566-412-3

Invitations to Inquiry

Why do ducks quack in the rain?
Do they think they'll get a grain?
Life's a riddle wrapped in jest,
Asking questions, we're all guests.

Why does cheese smell, yet taste divine?
It confounds, like the clock's design.
We ponder on each curious rhyme,
While time giggles, wasting time.

Embracing the Unknown

Jump into chaos, it's a thrill!
Who needs a map or a skill?
Wander lost but find delight,
In every twist, oh what a sight!

Why does ice cream fall from cones?
It seems life prefers our groans.
Chase the drip and laugh out loud,
While the universe plays the crowd.

Songs of Perplexity

Strumming chords on a soggy string,
Conversations dance, but never cling.
Why do socks disappear, I ask?
Life's odd puzzle, a silly task!

Searching for answers in lost shoes,
On this merry-go-round of blues.
With laughter echoing in the void,
Unsolved mysteries, never avoid!

Threads of Confusion

Why does cereal float in milk?
Like a boat made of soft silk?
Life's a quilt of mismatched threads,
Sewn with laughter, stitched with dread.

Tangled stories on the line,
Like old spoons without a shine.
In the chaos, we find our way,
With shimmying laughs leading the play.

A Jigsaw Without Pieces

A puzzle laid upon the floor,
But half of it is missing more.
I search for edges, seek the hues,
Yet find I can't decide on blues.

With corners lost, I scratch my head,
What was that piece? Or was it bread?
I laugh and sigh, what a delight,
Life's a game without a right.

Searching for Stars

I point to skies, and squint and stare,
  Expecting wisdom floating there.
But all I see are clouds and fluff,
  The universe can be so tough.

Perhaps the stars are playing hide,
  Behind a veil of cosmic pride.
I trip on thoughts that dance around,
Wishing for peace that's never found.

Beneath a Canopy of Questions

Underneath leaves of endless doubt,
I ponder, scream, then wander about.
The squirrels seem wise, with their chatter,
While my big queries just shatter.

Do fish have thoughts while swimming free?
Does grass feel joy or just agree?
I'm tangled up in all that's said,
While trees just nod and shake their heads.

Tangles in the Mind

My brain's a maze of silly schemes,
With dreams and thoughts like wobbly beams.
I chase a plot that goes astray,
Then find I've wandered far away.

It's like a dance but with two left feet,
A chaotic tune, yet oh so sweet.
I chuckle loud, what else to do?
Life's a riddle with a view.

Flickers of Revelation

In the kitchen, pots go bang,
My cat thinks it's a game.
Life's a jigsaw, missing pieces,
And I can't find my name.

Jokes in shadows, laughter fades,
Trying to peel an orange,
But it hurts my mind more than hands,
Maybe I'll just binge watch a range.

Wisdom comes and goes like storms,
While socks vanish in the dryer.
I ponder if ice cream's a food,
Or just a sweet desire.

So I dance with questions unasked,
Like a chicken on a line.
With humor as my daily mask,
I laugh at my own decline.

Dreams on a Tangled Path

I wander through a maze of thoughts,
With briars in my head.
Each corner turned, a riddle caught,
What should I have read?

Kites flutter in the restless breeze,
And my plans fly out of sight.
Should I chase my wayward keys,
Or just admire the flight?

Knocks at the door, but I don't greet,
Is it fate or a prank?
Life's a puzzle not complete,
As I forget the crank.

Sometimes I just sit and stare,
At cereal on my plate.
Do I toast to life or despair?
Let me just contemplate.

Chasing the Elusive Light

I follow sparks like shiny stars,
With sneakers tied too tight.
Chasing whims and chocolate bars,
In the dead of night.

Questions circle like a fly,
Buzzing in my ear.
What's the punchline? I won't lie,
I haven't got a clear.

A goldfish swims in circles grand,
While I munch on stale chips.
Is existence just being bland,
Or something that truly flips?

I flag down hope like a taxi,
But it drives right on past.
I chuckle, life's just a rapscallion,
A riddle, a jest, a blast.

Threads of Curiosity

In a web of thoughts I'm caught,
Like a fly on a spree.
Every answer comes with naught,
Just more, "What's left of me?"

Spinning tales around my room,
With a blanket for a cape.
I'm seeking answers in the gloom,
But mostly just escape.

A squirrel mocks my grand designs,
As it steals from my stash.
With each twist, a riddle shines,
At this point, I just laugh.

Through the haze, I chuckle bright,
Life's a joke, a tease.
In the dark, I find delight,
With quirks that never cease.

Fables of the Uncertain

In a world of questions, we stumble and run,
Searching for answers, we just can't outrun.
Life's a riddle wrapped tight in a joke,
Every deep thought's a punchline we poke.

From starlit wishes to coffee spills,
We ponder big dreams while chasing our thrills.
Maps drawn in crayons, the paths that we take,
Stepping on gum, oh the mess that we make!

We sip our confusion like fine aged wine,
Toast to the chaos, it's all so divine.
Each turn's a new story, or maybe a fable,
Life's just a parody, flip on the cable.

With every bright sunrise, we laugh at the grind,
The more that we ponder, the less we're aligned.
But hey, in the madness, let's dance and be free,
For the best part of life is the joy of the spree.

The Blank Slate of Existence

Waking up daily to a fresh pair of socks,
Searching for wisdom in shoeboxes and blocks.
Moments are fleeting, like ice cream in sun,
Savor it quickly, or you'll miss out on fun.

Questions like clouds drift across a blue sky,
Gathering thoughts as we wander nearby.
Each little mystery, like socks in the wash,
Bobblehead answers make us all want to gawk.

With giggles and chuckles, we roll through our days,
Untangling puzzles in all sorts of ways.
Life's a bizarre game of hide-and-seek bliss,
Much like a cat, it often goes amiss.

Frogs in tuxedos, dancing for glee,
Chasing down answers that never agree.
So let's raise a glass to the questions we find,
For happiness blooms in the fun we unwind.

The Map with No Destination

I unfolded a map, so bright and bold,
With X marks the spot, or so I was told.
Wandered through jungles, crossed rivers wide,
But all I found was my sandwich, fried.

Every turn pointed somewhere quite absurd,
The compass just laughed, no clear path occurred.
Chasing my shadow, round and round I went,
Turns out my heart is where time is spent.

Threads of Confusion

I tangled my thoughts like a ball of string,
Knots that turn tighter, what chaos they bring.
When I pull on a thread, it laughs in my face,
Says, 'Keep on pulling, you're losing the race!'

Each idea I grasped slipped right through my hands,
Winds of confusion blew over my plans.
Yet still I tie knots, though they tangle and twist,
Maybe life's just a game of a cutely named list.

Faces of the Infinite

I gazed at the stars, so much to explore,
Each twinkling light showed me even more lore.
But with every face, they wink in delight,
Leaving me puzzled if wrong or if right.

Questions come rushing, like waves on the shore,
What's up with the moon? Why's it keeping score?
An infinite puzzle where answers are rare,
But at least we can laugh and pretend we care.

Dancing with Ambiguity

In a ballroom of questions, I twirled with delight,
With partners of doubt, we danced through the night.
Each step that we took led to giggles and sighs,
What a curious waltz, under wayward skies.

With ambiguity leading my whimsical feet,
I stumbled and fumbled, couldn't find the beat.
Yet laughter erupted, a synchronized whirl,
Life's just a party—let's give it a twirl!

Whispers of Uncertainty

In the cafe, I ponder wide,
With a muffin, hard to decide.
Life's menu offers much to chew,
But every dish just leaves me blue.

Is it fortune? Or maybe fate?
I await guidance, but it's late.
With each sip, questions swirl in my cup,
What if I'm just a setup for a hiccup?

Echoes in the Abyss

Standing on the edge of thought,
Fearing the answers I have sought.
Like a sock that vanished in a wash,
Meaning has made its great nosh.

Echoes bounce with a chuckle and cheer,
But they're just polite—ah, they're not here.
Do I dive deep or stay afloat?
My brain's a boat that won't stay remote.

Navigating the Unknown

With a map drawn in crayon bright,
I set sail into the night.
The compass spins—a classic joke,
Is that a sign of hope or smoke?

Stars giggle, lighting up the skies,
But each twinkle just spins more lies.
Should I laugh or shed a tear?
In this maze, it's hard to steer.

Questions in the Silence

Silence screams in awkward tones,
Like a jammed phone that never moans.
I ask myself, with all my might,
Is it wrong to seek the light?

Friends nod fiercely, a motley crew,
Sharing cookies, yet no clue.
In this cosmic game, we play along,
Hoping to find where we belong.

Whispers in the Void

In the cosmic dance of fate,
Stars giggle and contemplate.
Clouds pass by with sarcastic cheer,
While I just sip my root beer.

Rabbits hop through the unknown,
Wearing hats like kings on their throne.
They wink at me with playful grace,
As I fumble through this endless space.

Jelly beans fall from the sky,
Time flies by with a wink and a sigh.
But here I stand with a puzzled mind,
Chasing answers I can't seem to find.

Life's a joke that we all play,
With punchlines lost on the way.
So let's share a laugh and let it go,
After all, we're just part of the show!

The Puzzle of Existence

Life's a jigsaw, missing pieces,
More questions grow as my brain increases.
I flip the box, read the hilarious blurb,
But wisdom's nowhere; it's all quite absurd.

Cats give me the side-eye glance,
While people ask me to join their dance.
But my two left feet stomp on the floor,
And I just trip over my own metaphor.

Socks get lost in the dryer of fate,
Bananas peel for the perfect date.
But why do they call it a cherry on top?
When my sundae just might bottom flop!

Is the cake really a lie, or truth?
I ponder this in my youth.
Between giggles, I take a stand,
And embrace chaos with a silly hand.

Questions Beneath the Surface

Why do ducks quack when they fly?
Where does all the leftover pie?
Do socks ever dream of being a pair?
While I'm stuck here without a spare.

The goldfish swims with a knowing grin,
Winking at me, where do I begin?
As I ponder the meaning behind a blink,
Counting bubbles makes me rethink.

Turtles race with lightning speed,
While I just sit, pondering my needs.
Life's riddles come and go at will,
Like tumbleweeds down a random hill.

In the chaos of thoughts that collide,
I laugh at the questions I cannot glide.
So let's toast to confusion's delight,
With a glass of juice, raising it high and bright!

Dancing on a Thread

Balancing life on a spider's string,
I twirl and leap, hoping to cling.
But one little slip sends me flying,
While butterflies giggle, no use denying.

The universe chuckles, a cosmic tease,
As I juggle lemons and try to appease.
Each fruit is a question, sour or sweet,
Trying to find rhythm with my flailing feet.

Clouds drift by, whispering schemes,
While I ponder my wild, tangled dreams.
Am I the dancer or part of the stage?
A cunning conundrum as I turn the page.

So here's to the dance we all share,
Wobbling on threads with plenty to spare.
Let's laugh at the circus of life we parade,
In the end, it's the jokes that we made!

Reflections on the Brink

I gazed into the mirror's face,
A question met me, wrapped in lace.
"What's the deal with all this strife?"
I shrugged; it's just a frolicking life.

In skies of blue, with clouds of gray,
I ponder loudly, then drift away.
The coffee spills, the cat just yawns,
Maybe meaning's found in dawns and fawns.

But then the phone rings, what a bore,
It's life calling, with laundry galore.
I'll chase the answers, oh what a game,
Until I realize, it's all the same!

So here I stand, a jesters' grin,
Balancing thoughts like a circus spin.
When laughed out loud, the questions fade,
In this wild ride, I'm glad I stayed.

Life's Tenuous Threads

A puppet on strings that dance and sway,
Attempting to find my quirky way.
The cosmic joke? I missed the punchline,
Chasing rainbows with socks that don't align.

What's the point of all this strife?
Maybe it's just picking up the knife.
To slice the cake of hope and doubt,
Laughing with friends, we figure it out.

Like spaghetti tangled on the floor,
Twisting and turning, always wanting more.
The meaning? A plate of pasta, undone,
Twirl it around, and you'll see it's fun!

So I raise my glass to the muddled paths,
And dance to the sound of life's silly laughs.
In the chaos, a cautious cheer,
Finding joy in the unclear.

Fleeting Truths

Why search for answers in a crowded room?
When the pizza rolls, and the laughter blooms.
Truths like smoke, they come and they go,
Dancing around like a clown on a show.

I tried to grasp it, a slippery fish,
With googly eyes and an ambitious wish.
Instead, I tripped on a cat's long tail,
Maybe life's meaning is to prevail!

So here's to absurdity, my old friend,
Spinning in circles, no start, no end.
I'll laugh with my doubts like they're alright,
Chasing the moon until the morning light.

Every question leads to more confusion,
Navigating life without institution.
The only truth, a chuckle or two,
In the silly spin of this crazy view.

Existence: An Open Question

I woke up today, just like last week,
Pondering life while I search for my peak.
A breakfast of nothing, but toast on the side,
Unraveling mysteries like I'm on a ride.

Life's an enigma wrapped in a flake,
Like a soggy crouton in a grand mistake.
Outrunning sighs on a treadmill of cheer,
What's back there, buddy, who's steering the pier?

So I dance on the edge of reason and rhyme,
In the land where nonsense commits the crime.
With giggles and snacks sparkling the day,
Maybe the answers just enjoy the play.

An open question, I toast with delight,
To finding joy in the quirkiness of life.
With a wink and a smirk, I'll wander along,
In this silly search, I'll hum my own song.

Embracing the Great Unknown

In the maze of thoughts, I roam,
Searching high and low for a home.
Questions dance like bees in the air,
But answers vanish—never there.

With maps and charts, I set my quest,
But every clue leaves me less than blessed.
I trip on riddles, fall in the muck,
And since when did 'why' mean 'good luck'?

The stars align, or so they say,
But my GPS lost its way.
Each twist and turn brings puzzled glee,
Hey, is that a goat, or just a tree?

Through laughter, I wade in the stream,
Life's strange waves are quite the theme.
So, I'll join the dance, come what may,
In confusion's arms, I'll sway away.

Searching for Shadows

I peek around and search for clues,
Life's big puzzle has odd views.
I chase my tail, a merry game,
But finding sense? Oh, what a shame!

Shadows whisper, secrets tease,
They say the answer's in the breeze.
I sniff and hunt, and what do I find?
A rubber chicken? Was that intertwined?

With pockets full of sticky notes,
I scribble dreams while wearing coats.
Life's absurdity gives me a nod,
Does that mean I'm some sort of god?

But as I stumble, grin on my face,
I embrace the chaos, feel its grace.
For in this whirlwind of fun and jest,
Maybe nonsense is simply the best!

Echoes of Uncertainty

In the depths of my muddled mind,
Echoes of why softly remind.
I toss and turn, can't sleep a wink,
Maybe coffee's the answer? I think.

With friends, we ponder, sip, and stare,
The meaning of life? Who would dare?
We joke and laugh, the truth feels far,
Like chasing dreams in a fast-moving car.

Philosophers may strut and pose,
But I find meaning in my toes.
Tickling them leads to fits of glee,
Who knew the answer could be so free?

So here I stand, arms open wide,
In this mystery, I take my stride.
Life's riddles amusingly unfold,
As I embrace the silliness, bold and gold!

Pieces of a Mysterious Puzzle

In a box marked with question marks,
Lies a jigsaw of baffling quirks.
Every piece is a different face,
Glue them together? No such grace.

One's a cat, another's a shoe,
Does it fit? I haven't a clue!
Colors clash with wild delight,
Yet somehow, it feels just right.

I search for answers in a pile,
With every turn, I lose my style.
It all seems a cosmic joke,
Maybe I'm destined for a poke.

So here I sit, with puzzle bits,
Laughing at life's unusual fits.
If each piece were a lesson learned,
I guess I'm just here, still concerned!

Shadows of Doubt

In the corner lurks a shadowy doubt,
Whispers of 'what are you about?'
It nudges me to change my course,
Yet makes me laugh—oh, what a force!

I ponder deep with a furrowed brow,
Contemplating if I should allow
This little specter to dictate fate,
Or tell it to leave—I've got a date!

Should I dance with shadows in the night?
Or just stay home, switch on the light?
For every worry that taps my shoulder,
I giggle and say, 'Ooh, do come bolder!'

So here's to doubt, my quirky friend,
Let's toast to questions that never end.
With every laugh, it loses its sting,
Maybe doubt is just life's fun fling!

A Journey Through the Unseen

I packed my bags for a trip unknown,
With snacks and dreams, all rolled into one.
But the map just giggles—no roads are shown,
Off I go, feeling light as a bun.

Each corner I turn, another surprise,
A family of squirrels in sunglasses fly.
They point to the void, saying, 'Look, see?'
Is this where I'm meant to be?

I wander through clouds of sugary fluff,
Life's a carnival, isn't it tough?
With every ride, my laughter explodes,
Yet I trip on the path, and it erodes.

So I chase the breeze, and I float along,
In this journey of whimsy, I belong.
A tale so funny, it spins my soul,
Who needs a guide when you're on a roll?

Reflections in a Broken Mirror

I peek into shards of shattered glass,
A thousand faces stare back with sass.
Some grinning wide, some frowning low,
Do they know something? I just don't know!

Each crack tells a riddle, a story unspun,
Of wild adventures and days full of fun.
Yet there's my mug, looking quite lost,
Do mirrors have feelings? Oh, what a cost!

With patches of laughter and scars made of cheer,
Every blemish reflects a truth—oh, dear!
Do I take the time to fuse it back clear,
Or embrace the chaos, sip on a beer?

In pieces I stand, with sparkle and grime,
Finding beauty in chaos, each twist of time.
So let's raise a toast to all that is strange,
Life's a mess and it's fabulously deranged!

Shadows Cast by Doubt

In a world of big questions,
I'm lost in the fluff.
Pondering existence,
But it feels rather tough.

I asked my goldfish,
What's the deal with this life?
He just circled his bowl,
Free from all strife.

I tried to get answers,
From my cat on the bed.
But he stretched and yawned,
And then went back to red.

So I laugh at my worries,
With a wink and a nod.
Perhaps we're all clueless,
Just a bit like a fraud.

The Paradox of Being

I woke up in a haze,
With questions galore.
Why are we here, I ask,
Beyond bedroom floor?

The toaster chimed loudly,
As my toast took a leap.
It popped and it burned,
But my thoughts aren't too deep.

I ponder my purpose,
With a donut in hand.
Does life need a reason,
Or is it just bland?

I joke with my coffee,
As it spills on my shirt.
He's got deep aspirations,
While I just feel hurt.

Stories Yet to be Told

In the library of life,
Dusty shelves full of dreams.
I searched for the answers,
But nothing's as it seems.

I met a wise old sage,
Who talked under the sun.
He said life is a puzzle,
But forgot to bring one.

Each story left untold,
Twists like spaghetti strands.
I tripped over my thoughts,
Just like my clumsy hands.

So I laugh at my quest,
With each silly mistake.
Maybe it's funnier,
Than the truth we could make.

Fractured Ideals

I scribbled my dreams,
On a napkin today.
But the ink ran all wild,
And just washed away.

My plans looked so grand,
Until they fell apart.
Like my youth on a roller,
To the beat of the heart.

I chased after wisdom,
Like a dog on a run.
But wisdom just giggled,
Said, 'Aren't we all fun?'

So here's to the chaos,
And the laughter we find.
Life's riddle remains,
But it's one of a kind.

Riddles of Reality

Why do we laugh when we should cry?
The pizza's hot, but so am I.
Lost keys in pockets, I try to seek,
Life's a game of hide-and-peek.

Cats chase tails in a circus show,
Have you seen my socks? I'll never know.
Each question asked, a new surprise,
Like juggling jellybeans in the skies.

Dreams are whispers, or so they say,
Like trying to catch a cloud at play.
An orange elephant in the room,
Who invited this? It's lost its bloom.

So here's to the questions we can't resolve,
Like a puzzle box that's hard to solve.
Life's a riddle, with laughs and sighs,
Kiss your confusion—give it a rise!

Explorations in Grey

In shades of grey, I sip my tea,
What's the answer? You'll just see.
A goat on a roof? It's plain absurd,
Yet here I stand, unbothered, unheard.

Cloudy decisions hover in my mind,
With thoughts like spaghetti, all intertwined.
Do fishes get thirsty? They've no clue,
So let's swim in circles—just me and you.

A dance with shadows, a twirl in the dark,
Searching for meaning, I found a spark.
Why do we ponder what we can't explain?
Life's just a game of chasing the rain.

So let's celebrate mischief and jest,
In this wild world, humor's the best.
With mismatched socks and playful grins,
I'll laugh while I wonder where life begins!

The Handshake with Ambiguity

A handshake with doubt feels quite bizarre,
Like riding a bicycle built for a star.
Do ducks play poker? I've not a clue,
But if they did, I'd join them too.

Embracing chaos, we spin and twirl,
In a world of giggles, let loose and swirl.
Counting the jellybeans on a shelf,
Just maybe they'll hold the secret of self.

Now, what's the point of this silly rant?
Like searching for treasure in a disheveled plant.
Every question leads to more delight,
So let's toast to confusion, stars, and flight.

As we shake hands with all that's unclear,
I smile at the mystery, let's grab a beer.
In the end, there's humor in the unknown,
Dancing with shadows, never alone!

Contours of Curiosity

Curiosity piqued, I wander outside,
Through fields of whimsy, on fate's bumpy ride.
Why do squirrels wear tiny frowns?
Perhaps they know the secrets of towns.

Mapping my thoughts like a treasure map,
In a world where nonsense decides to clap.
Do plants gossip while sipping the rain?
They whisper sweet nothings, not much to gain.

A curious cat prowls in the night,
With dreams of fish that glide in flight.
Who's to say what's real or a dream?
As I laugh at my thoughts, bursting at the seam.

So here's to the wanderers, brave and bright,
Who chase after shadows and dance with light.
In the frolic of questions, we find our glee,
Laughing at life's grand mystery!

Musings in the Twilight

In the dusk of thought, I ponder,
What's the reason for yonder?
A cat's meow, a dog's glare,
Do they reveal truths we wouldn't dare?

Life's a riddle wrapped in cheer,
Banana peels bring the truth near.
But I slip and fall, lose my way,
Chasing dreams that seem to stray.

A juggling clown in a top hat,
Says life's just a game of pat-a-cake.
I nod along, though I suspect,
He stole my thoughts, what the heck?

As night falls down, I chuckle loud,
With all these questions, I'm quite proud.
But deep inside, I can't ignore,
Answers hide behind the door.

The Canvas of Questions

Brush strokes flying, chaos reigns,
Colors blend with ghostly chains.
Why's purple sad while yellow laughs?
Maybe it's art's remarkable gaffs.

A canvas blank, my mind's alike,
With questions circling like a bike.
Pedal faster, please don't stop,
Finding sense within this crop.

I painted a sun, it turned to cheese,
Which makes me giggle, if you please.
Artistry blends in the oddest way,
Especially on a confused Tuesday.

Yet here I stand with brush in hand,
Creating meaning, or was it planned?
If life's a canvas full of quirks,
Then grab your paints, and let's do the jerks!

Between Reality and Illusion

Is this real, or just a dream?
I'm sipping coffee with a meme.
The spoon's a fork, the wall's a mouse,
Welcome to my wacky house!

Mirrors lie with perfect grace,
Reflecting thoughts that meander space.
Is that me, or just a clone?
Let's make a toast with cupcakes blown!

Illusions dance like butterflies,
Twirling truths in crazy skies.
As shadows whisper sweet nothings near,
I just laugh, with a hint of fear.

So here I stand, an enigma rare,
Between what's real and unreal flair.
Who needs answers, let's just play,
In this curious game of all-day sway!

Beyond the Horizon of Understanding

Set sail on dreams, all hands on deck,
Searching for sense in a life unchecked.
With maps made out of candy canes,
And compasses that jive with trains.

Beyond the horizon, questions float,
Like rubber ducks in a silly moat.
Each wave a giggle, each splash a grin,
Who knew wisdom was this akin?

Clouds shaped like cats and fish parade,
As I ponder the choices made.
But laughter's the light that guides me true,
In this wondrous view, oh, who knew?

So let's hoist the sails of absurd delight,
Navigating life's silly plight.
With every heartbeat, we'll just go,
Past horizons where answers will overflow!

Paths to Nowhere

I took a stroll on a sunny day,
With a map that led me astray.
Every turn felt oh-so-right,
But I found myself lost by night.

I asked for directions, no one knew,
They pointed me towards the zoo.
So I chuckled, embraced the quirk,
As a monkey gave me a smirk.

Life's a journey, or so they say,
I just keep missing the freeway.
Maybe paths to nowhere are fun,
At least I've met a lot of puns!

So here I wander, a detour king,
Alive with giggles, I let joy sing.
No destination, just the thrill,
A path of laughter, and that's the deal!

To Live Without Certainty

I wake each day with coffee in hand,
Dripping thoughts like grains of sand.
My future's a puzzle with missing parts,
But I wear my confusion like art.

I flip a coin for big decision,
Heads, I try; tails, I vision.
My life's a sitcom, laugh tracks on cue,
It's perfectly fine, I have no clue!

Should I buy a plant or leave it be?
I'll water it — or could it be me?
Quite a mystery, this everyday plight,
As I ponder with glee, under soft sunlight.

At last, understanding has made its retreat,
But I'm dancing on toes, feeling light on my feet.
Life's jokes play out without any scripts,
And in this madness, I'm taking my trips!

Beneath the Surface of Being

Beneath the ripples of daily grind,
Lurks a fish with a curious mind.
It might ask, 'What's the point of it all?'
Then promptly forgets, as it swims with a ball.

The depths of my thoughts are like murky lakes,
Where I stash memories and giggly mistakes.
Some say I'm profound, but really I'm jest,
Just a clown in a riddle, on a life quest.

I ponder the chaos, the noise, the smirk,
And wonder if chocolate is true work.
Surfaces glimmer, but what lies down deep?
Oh look, a catfish! I'll add it to my keep.

Through watery lenses, life's a grand show,
With laughter and quirks, it's a comedic flow.
So here's to the depths, where bubbles rise high,
Let's toast to confusion, let silly times fly!

The Weight of Wonder

Weighed down by questions, I ponder and sigh,
Is there a reason? I just ask the sky.
With stars twinkling back, I squint with glee,
Should I get half a sandwich or just let it be?

Each riddle presents with a wink and a grin,
While life shows me dance moves, I ponder within.
Should I tango with knowledge or hop with a tune?
I think I'll just waddle like a silly cartoon.

The burden of wisdom a true heavy pack,
But a giggler's light heart knows no sense of lack.
I'll wade through the musings, no heavy regrets,
With laughter as currency, I'm cashing in bets!

So here's to the weight of our whimsical minds,
To questions and quandaries, feel free to unwind.
Life's a big jest, where seriousness slips,
Let's raise a glass to the joy of our trips!

Fleeting Facets of Existence

Life is but a fleeting show,
Like shadows dancing to and fro.
We search for answers, yet we roam,
In the circus of the unknown.

A cat in a hat on a pogo stick,
Spouts wisdom that's quite the trick.
While we ponder and scratch our heads,
He just naps on the riches of beds.

With each new dawn comes a fresh surprise,
Like a magician in disguise.
We juggle questions, laugh and weep,
While meaning takes a strange, odd leap.

So let's toast to the great unknown,
A puzzle wrapped in a rolling stone.
We may not solve it, that's quite clear,
But what fun we'll have while we're here!

The Canvas of Questions

A blank canvas, paintbrush in hand,
Scribbling nonsense, oh isn't life grand?
Colors of doubt and shades of delight,
Splashing across the day and night.

What's the secret, the ultimate scheme?
Is existence just a bizarre dream?
A penguin in a tux, quite sublime,
Sips tea while we lose track of time.

Questions dance like butterflies bold,
In a field of stories yet untold.
With every flick, we chuckle and sigh,
As answers flit just out of our eye.

Perplexity is our constant friend,
Through this labyrinth, we twist and bend.
Embrace the chaos, revel in jest,
For life's a riddle, at best, not a test!

Oracle of the Infinite

In the land of what-ifs, we'll take a stroll,
Where the wise old sage plays the jester's role.
With riddles and rhymes, he'll lead the way,
To a throne made of questions, so come, let's play.

"Why are we here?" we fervently ask,
As he grins, "Well, that's quite the task!
But here's a secret, if you must know,
It's mostly just chance—put on a show!"

The oracle chuckles, pouring tea,
As we sip on life's sweet mystery.
With biscuits and banter, we ponder anew,
What it all means, if it means anything too.

Yet in the laughter, the crux is found,
Like a zany dance, twirling 'round and 'round.
We may not get it, that's quite alright,
For the journey's a party, in day or night!

Storms of Inquiry

Thunder rolls in with a question fair,
As lightning zaps thoughts through the air.
"A purpose, a reason?" we all inquire,
While umbrellas flip in this playful mire.

Chasing answers like squirrels at play,
Searching for meaning in such a fray.
Yet as the winds howl and the rain pours down,
We laugh it off, donning puddle caps crowned.

For who can catch raindrops, slippery and fast?
With each drop that falls, we find a new cast.
Life's a tempest of cheers and jeers,
Waltzing through storms with light-hearted peers.

So let's dance in the rain and embrace the unknown,
In the whirlwind of chaos, we've truly grown.
If answers evade, let's giggle and sway,
For life's biggest question is just how to play!

Searching for the Hidden Compass

I searched for guidance in a map,
But found a donut instead, a tasty trap.
Directions scribbled in icing neat,
I took a bite, life's conundrums sweet.

With every fork and twist I take,
A compass spins, oh what a mistake!
Is north a feeling or a place?
I've lost my way in this sugary pace.

I asked a squirrel for some advice,
It winked and ran, oh so precise.
Can wisdom wear a fuzzy coat?
Or is it found in the songs of a goat?

In laughter shared, I find my light,
A compass hidden in silly delight.
If life's a puzzle, I'll make it fun,
With chocolate chips and a dash of pun.

Paradoxes of Existence

Why do we run when we've nowhere to go?
In loops we dance, like a dog chasing snow.
The more we strive, the less we succeed,
Are we planting roots or chasing the lead?

With questions that tickle and thoughts that play,
I trip on my shoelaces, hey, that's my way!
Life's a riddle wrapped in a hopeful sigh,
Like finding your sock in the pie of a pie.

In dinner conversations, we find our muse,
Yelling 'Eureka!' when we just mean 'Excuse!'
The universe chuckles, a cosmic jester,
As we ponder the hows while dressing for the festa.

So grab a slice of the absurd today,
Laugh at the chaos that dances our way.
For life is a jest, a grand little prank,
Let's raise our glasses for all that we thank.

The Enigma of Purpose

I woke one morn with a grand to-do,
To solve my purpose, what's life's big view?
With coffee brewing and socks all mismatched,
I questioned the cosmos, the stars haphazardly patched.

I pondered a cactus, so prickly yet free,
Does it seek to bloom or just be a tree?
With every second, the world spins fast,
Yet here I sit, stuck in breakfast cast.

The cat on the rug seems to get it right,
Napping through answers, with pure feline might.
I asked its opinion, amidst purrs and stretches,
It blinked at me slowly, then turned with great sketches.

Let's toast to the questions, the quirks of our fate,
For life's not a puzzle but a jumbled crate.
With laughter as fuel and love as our guide,
We'll dance through the mystery with joy as our stride.

Fleeting Moments of Clarity

Sometimes in shower steam, ideas appear,
Like bubbles of thought, pop—then they're clear!
The wisdom of ducks in a park makes me cheer,
But just like that, poof!—distraction draws near.

I wrote down my insights, a sage with a pen,
But spilled my juice, and now it's all zen.
Do we learn from the mess or cling to the neat?
Life's full of chaos, like ants in a heat.

Once I saw meaning in the way that they dance,
But tripped on my shoes, lost my dreamy romance.
Maybe enlightenment slips through our hands,
Mixing with laughter while joyfully planned.

So here's to the moments that tickle our brains,
That nudge us to giggle through life's silly lanes.
In light and in shadows, in topsy-turvy knots,
We'll find our own truth in the laughter it spots.

The Silent Quest

In the search for wisdom, I tripped on a shoe,
I asked a wise old owl, he just hooted, who knew?
Gazing at the stars, I pondered my fate,
Found a donut in the grass, life's treats can wait.

Chasing after answers, I caught a quick breeze,
The clouds just giggled, the sun teased with ease.
I asked a wandering cat, reclining in shade,
She licked her paw and said, 'I'm just getting laid.'

I followed a squirrel, he darted up high,
Mumbling profound thoughts, he whispered, 'Just try!'
But I fell in a puddle, my dreams washed away,
A rubber duck grinned and said, 'Don't forget to play!'

Now I dance with confusion, a grand masquerade,
The meaning's a riddle, a game yet to be played.
So I giggle and wiggle, with questions on hold,
Life's quirks keep me guessing, and that never gets old.

Mysteries of a Fleeting Moment

Time made a salad, tossed in some dread,
A squirt of confusion, with thoughts lightly spread.
I chewed on a lemon, it wrinkled my frown,
A circus of moments, like a clown in a gown.

Owls give advice; they've seen all that's true,
But I got sidetracked by a kangaroo crew.
They danced in a line, hopping high as can be,
Said, 'Life's just a riddle, come live it with me!'

I peek under rocks for profound wisdom's gold,
Only found a worm, slimy stories untold.
A butterfly flitted, whispered in my ear,
'Life's brief like my flutter, but oh, so sincere!'

In the jigsaw of chaos, I laughed at the strife,
Searching for meaning, I found slices of life.
With each little giggle, I store it away,
Moments are fleeting, so let's dance and play.

Labyrinth of Doubts

In a maze made of questions, where answers hide tight,
I bumped into a puppy, who barked at my plight.
He seemed to know things, with a wag of his tail,
But guess what? He chased a squirrel, and off he set sail.

I wandered through corridors of slippery thought,
Found myself in a corner, with wisdom I sought.
A wise old goat chewing grass with delight,
Said, 'Just nibble on life, don't fuss about right!'

The walls often whispered—a chorus of fear,
While jellybeans giggled, 'Just move in good cheer!'
I tumbled through riddles that juggled my mind,
And danced with my doubts, an odd friend I'd find.

So in this grand labyrinth, I'll stumble and spin,
Each turn is a lesson, where laughter begins.
As I trip through the doubts, I'll sing silly songs,
And learn life's absurdity is where my heart belongs.

Fragments of Understanding

I pieced it together, a puzzling old game,
Each bit a banana, too slippery to claim.
Surrounded by mirrors that echo my face,
Each reflection chuckles, 'You're lost in this place!'

I asked for directions from a wise old tree,
It waved its branches, like 'Don't bother me!'
Amidst the confusions, I laughed at my quest,
'Just wing it!' chirped a bird, as it took a short rest.

With fragments of laughter, I try to conjoin,
But life's like a puzzle where none fits the coin.
A shadow passed by with a dance and a twirl,
It said, 'Just embrace it, this mad little whirl!'

So I gather my bits as I frolic and roam,
With each little mishap, I make my own home.
In the chaos and chuckles, I'm finding my way,
Embracing the nonsense, come join in the play!

Pilgrimage Without Purpose

I set out with a map in hand,
A compass spinning, oh so grand,
With every turn, I lost my way,
But hey, it made for a fun day!

I met a duck who quacked profound,
Said wisdom's lost where laughs abound,
I nodded, and we shared a snack,
Now I can't remember what I lack!

The mountains loomed like giant beans,
While clouds above played hide and seeks,
I chased a butterfly so spry,
And pondered if I'd learned to fly.

But as I wandered night and morn,
I realized I was quite forlorn,
Yet laughter bubbled up like soda,
Leaving me in a puzzling moda!

Glimmers of Insight

A chicken crossed to find the truth,
It scratched its head, what is the proof?
All that I learned from fowl and friends,
Is life's a joke with no clear ends.

I stared at clouds that shaped my fate,
But found they looked just like a plate,
With pizza slices—where's the spice?
I guess the universe ate my slice!

The sun might rise, but so does my bed,
Dreams are more fun than thoughts in my head,
I laugh at stars for shining too bright,
And wonder if they sleep at night.

As years go by, I scribble notes,
On napkins, shirts, and empty coats,
I hope one day I'll find a clue,
But maybe laughs are the best we do!

Meandering through Moments

I stroll through life with mismatched shoes,
Each step I take, a different muse,
A kid on a swing, soaring so free,
Yelling, "What's the point? Can it be me?"

A squirrel paused—its acorn a prize,
I asked it why it's so wise,
It twirled and danced, then ran up a tree,
I marveled, could it teach me glee?

Time slips through fingers like sand so fine,
Each grain a moment, a twist in the line,
I grinned at the winds that blew my hat,
Said, "Is this life? Or just a chat?"

I scribble thoughts on a paper plane,
Then watch it fly off, never to reign,
But laughter lingers, a sweet gentle tune,
Marking moments beneath the moon.

Embracing Ambivalence

I woke up today feeling quite mixed,
Like scrambled eggs without the fix,
Should I laugh or simply frown?
I chose to wear my clownish crown.

I danced with shadows, tangoed with fears,
Sipped lemonade with forgotten years,
Flip a coin, should I stay or should I roam?
The answer's lost somewhere near home.

A cat on a fence, sunbathing wide,
Whiskers twitching, the feline guide,
It winked at me, "Life's just a game,
So chase your tail, forget the fame!"

As I embrace this vibrant swirl,
With all its chaos that gives a twirl,
I giggle softly at the absurd,
For in confusion, wisdom stirred!

Unraveling the Knot of Being

Why quench the thirst for clues we seek,
A riddle wrapped in silly mystique.
I asked a wise man, he shrugged his gain,
And pointed me to a dancing crane.

Life's puzzle pieces, scattered and wild,
Giggles from a thoughtful child.
If wisdom's a game, I've lost my track,
Chasing shadows that always come back.

Questions sprout like weeds from the ground,
Answers play tag, never found.
So let's sit back and sip our tea,
Laughing at what's yet to be.

In this circus, we're merely clowns,
Tumbling about in colorful gowns.
Embrace the jest of what we don't know,
As life's grand show puts on a glow.

The Silence Between Answers

In the quiet, questions bloom wide,
Whispers of chaos that we can't abide.
I thought I knew, then lost the thread,
Now I'm a parrot, squawking instead.

Underneath my thinking cap,
Lies a brain like Swiss, full of gaps.
I asked the cat, it just purred back,
With wisdom wrapped in a fuzzy pack.

I brushed with truth, it played hide and seek,
Left me wondering, feeling quite weak.
Should I call a friend or just snack?
Maybe ponder this with a sweet little quack.

The silence hums a curious tune,
While contemplating life under the moon.
There's laughter in the unknown, oh yes,
Join me in this delightful mess!

Wandering Through Fables

Once upon a time in a wacky land,
Where questions danced like grains of sand.
I met a fox wearing stylish shoes,
Who laughed and danced, spreading the news.

In fables told with hints and flair,
The slice of truth floats in the air.
I chased it through a field of dreams,
Just to find it's bursting at the seams.

Tales twist and turn like vines on a wall,
Where answers giggle and play, not small.
I asked a tree with a wise old face,
It chuckled softly, "Life's a race!"

So come along, let's stroll the path,
With laughter trailing, and joy in our math.
The fables spin tales, who's to complain?
For laughter's the sunshine when it starts to rain.

The Art of Not Knowing

They say ignorance is bliss, how absurd!
But here I stand with a cheeky word.
Not knowing things makes me a champ,
In the carnival of thought, I'm the lamp.

With questions like balloons in the air,
I float around without a care.
Each guess a piece of candy, divine,
I pop them open and sip on the wine.

Philosophy? A mix-up of pie,
Slice it up, let the answers fly.
With wit as my guide, I trip and sway,
In the art of unsure, let's dance and play.

So here's to life's perfect little mess,
Embracing each giggle in the quest.
For in the void of knowing, I find a cheer,
Let's toast to fun, and steer clear of fear!

The Winding Road to Nowhere

I took a trip to find my place,
Only to end up face to face.
With a squirrel that stole my snack,
And a sign that pointed back.

I asked a tree, 'What should I do?'
It rustled leaves, but never grew.
My GPS lost, you see it's fine,
Just another twist in this grand design.

The mountain peaks turned out to be,
Just piles of dirt staring back at me.
I laughed and danced with ageless stones,
While pondering where I left my phone.

At each strange turn, I found a clue,
That maybe life's just peek-a-boo.
With every setback and every fall,
Maybe not knowing's the best of all.

Secrets Wrapped in Silence

Whispers float on the gentle breeze,
Promising answers with effortless ease.
But they giggle and vanish when I get near,
Just like my sock that disappears!

I asked a cat perched high on a wall,
'What's the point in this grand free-for-all?'
She licked her paw and stared at me,
As if life's puzzle's best left to be.

Chasing shadows, seeking the light,
I tripped over my thoughts in the night.
The moon just winked and said, 'Oh please,
Tell me again how you follow the breeze!'

So maybe the secrets are just a ruse,
Wrapped in laughter, an eternal cruise.
For life's a joke we all just share,
While searching for meaning in mid-air.

Making Sense of the Senseless

I once tried to count all the stars,
But lost track after counting to four.
Knowing I'd never find a sense,
I just giggled and tripped on the floor.

I wondered why fish don't wear shoes,
Or if clouds ever sing the blues.
With every ponder and every thought,
I failed to grasp what I ought.

I juggled my dreams with a spoon and a fork,
While chatting with friends who claim they're a stork.
We laughed at their feathers, bright and bold,
And spun tales of fortune that never unfold.

In this circus of life, we juggle and dance,
Hoping to find meaning, given the chance.
But sometimes the chaos is where the fun lies,
As we squint at the sky and continue to rise.

Echoes from the Abyss

In the abyss, I heard a call,
A voice that said, 'You'll never know all.'
I echoed back with a chuckle and grin,
'Guess it's true, let the chaos begin!'

I tossed my worries into the void,
And watched as they danced, feeling overjoyed.
The darkness chuckled, 'You silly fool,
Life's just a game, without a rule.'

Out in the cosmos, lost and unfound,
Time and space spun merrily around.
I tried to hold on to some grand insight,
But nothing quite landed, try as I might.

So here's to the echoes, they give me a cheer,
Reminding me nonsense is worth a good year.
For in this wild ride, strange and divine,
The laughter we share is simply sublime.

In the Silence of Unknowing

In the quiet of my mind, we chat,
But all I hear is an echoing splat.
Questions float like balloons in the air,
Laughing at me, they just don't care.

I searched for answers under my bed,
But found only crumbs and a sock instead.
The meaning hides like a prankster's face,
Sprinting away at a comical pace.

I asked the stars with a cosmic sigh,
But they twinkled back a confused 'Why?'
Life's puzzle pieces scattered and tossed,
A game where I'm always a little bit lost.

Yet here I am, dancing in the dark,
With giggles of joy like a bright spark.
Unknowing can lead to a whimsical spree,
Embracing the chaos, just let it be!

A Feather on the Breeze

A feather flutters, light and free,
Whispering secrets, teasing me.
"Life's a ride," it seems to chirp,
"Just hold on tight, don't be a burp!"

I chased that feather, oh what a sight,
It danced away in a playful flight.
Like life's answers, they wiggle and flee,
Leaving me wondering, what could they be?

Sometimes I ponder, should I just float,
On currents of whims, like an old boat?
Amusement drips from every unknown,
As I juggle my thoughts like a playful stone.

So here I am, caught in the breeze,
With laughter and joy, I feel so at ease.
If life's a mystery, a game of tease,
I'll take it with humor, if you please!

Reflections in a Broken Mirror

A mirror cracked with a funny face,
Shows me my doubts, in a twisted space.
I laugh at the fragments telling me lies,
Like a haunted funhouse, echoing sighs.

Each shard reflects a different story,
A comedy act without any glory.
Ask the pieces what wisdom they'll send,
But they just giggle and won't make amends.

I tiptoe around, stepping on dreams,
Every step echoes with absurd screams.
Hilarity blooms in the corridor of time,
Jokes on my journey, a whimsical rhyme.

In this broken glass, I see the light,
It's not about answers, but the sheer delight.
So I'll strut my stuff, eccentric and wild,
In life's quirky tales, forever a child!

The Color of Uncertainty

What hue is life? I'd love to know,
But colors blend in a merry-go.
The reds and blues laugh, play hide and seek,
As I trip on oranges like a silly freak.

I tried to paint my future bright,
But my brush strokes are a comical sight.
I asked a rainbow, all full of cheer,
It winked and said, "But which one, dear?"

In the land of hues, I roam around,
With shades of confusion, I'm glory-bound.
Every blending moment, a nuanced art,
Like a splatter of paint, straight from the heart.

So here's to uncertainty, a vivid spree,
The laughter it brings is wild and free.
Life's canvas may be a crazy mess,
But isn't that simply the best kind of jest?

Why Not Just Be?

Woke up today, felt quite absurd,
The world was a blur, no lines to be stirred.
Coffee in hand, I ponder and muse,
Why bother to stress? I think I'll just snooze.

The cat thinks she knows, she sleeps all day,
While I chase my tail in a comical way.
With laughter I giggle, at life's little jest,
Is it all just a game? I don't know, but it's best.

Why run in circles, when I can just float?
Instead of a roadmap, I'll use a small boat.
Drifting on whims, avoiding the grind,
Maybe just being is the best state of mind.

With ice cream for breakfast, let's up the degree,
If confusion's a dish, then I'll have a spree.
Life's big of a puzzle, in pieces we roam,
Why not just be? Turns out, it's a home.

The Art of Not Knowing

I've mastered the art; it's quite a delight,
To shrug off the answers and just feel alright.
With a sprinkle of chaos and dazzle of charm,
I'll dance to the rhythm, and hold on to calm.

Why worry 'bout paths when I can just drift?
Life's like a package, it's all a strange gift.
The questions are many, the answers so few,
I'll simply pretend that I've got a clear view.

Like skimming a book, I read only the jokes,
Life's full of surprises and whimsical pokes.
With a giggle or two, I shall navigate drear,
And laugh at the silliness, never show fear.

So here's to not knowing, a toast we'll raise high,
To the weirdness of life, oh me, oh my!
With humor as armor, I'll boldly explore,
The art of not knowing? I'm ready for more.

Navigating the Unknown

Maps are for dreamers, I'm lost with a grin,
In the maze of the mind is where fun can begin.
With a quirk of fate, and a dash of surprise,
Navigating the unknown, oh what a prize!

Twists and turns make it a wild little ride,
Like searching for treasures, I'll take them in stride.
Forget all the plans, let's just see what we find,
In the chaos of life, let's not be confined.

I'll hide from the answers, the facts, and the grind,
In the riddle of living, the joy's intertwined.
With laughter as my compass, I'll wander and roam,
Finding gems in the question, I'll call it my home.

So here's to the journeys that leave us agog,
With whimsy and wonders, I'll dance with the fog.
Navigating the unknown, for all it's worth,
I'll make it a party, a whimsical birth!

In Search of Answers

With a magnifying glass, I seek high and low,
For clues hidden 'round where the funny winds blow.
I ask all the wise, but they scratch their chin,
Maybe the answer's in cupcakes and gin?

With questions galore, I won't stop or pout,
I'll flip every stone, hear what's buzzing about.
Like a detective of yore, with a pipe and a hat,
I'll follow the riddles and laugh at the chat.

Perhaps I'll find wisdom in silly old jokes,
Or treasures in giggles over rich, fragrant smokes.
Each ponder a puzzle, each thought a balloon,
In search of the answers, I howl at the moon.

So if life is a riddle, I'll dance in its glow,
With laughter my guide, through the ebb and the flow.
In search of answers, I'll spark up the cheer,
For life's greatest mysteries still lead me to beer!

Inquiries of the Heart

Why is pizza round, but served in a square?
And socks disappear, like they just don't care.
I ponder my purpose, but then I just snack,
I place all my questions into a big sack.

Do fish really know about water's embrace?
Or is it just a confusing old race?
I wonder if clouds ever dream of the ground,
While I trip on my shoes that are loosely bound.

Why do cats stare like they own the whole room?
And why do we laugh, then succumb to the gloom?
Perhaps life is simply a jester's grand play,
Where meanings are hidden, then tossed away.

I chase all my thoughts, like they're butterflies,
But they flutter and flit, oh how time flies.
With questions aplenty, I dance in a blur,
And maybe the answer is just a good purr.

Beyond the Fathom

What goes through a dog's mind when I leave?
Do they think it's a game, or is there reprieve?
I ponder the stars and their twinkling charms,
While life's little hiccups throw me off my arms.

Why do we say 'break a leg' before shows?
Do wishes on dandelions ever suppose?
I toss all my thoughts like confetti in air,
Laughing at notions that life's just unfair.

Can squirrels be ninjas with acrobatic flair?
Or is that a question too wild to declare?
I muse about frogs in the rain's cute parade,
As I sit by the window, all happily swayed.

Perhaps it's the whimsy that color our days,
Or the chuckle we share in the silliest ways.
The meaning's elusive, like a pie in the sky,
But giggles and grins are the best reason why.

Chronicles of Ambiguity

Is it true that time waits for no little shoe?
Or does it just dance while we scramble for clues?
I laugh at the notion that life's a tight race,
While juggling my duties with cookie crumbs' grace.

Why do we say 'head over heels' in love?
Aren't we already portly, like a fat dove?
Each quirk of existence feels oddly surreal,
Like trying to teach a goldfish to feel.

What if the earth is just a giant balloon?
Popping in laughter, it floats to the moon?
I chase after thoughts that don't know where to land,
And wonder if life's just a game poorly planned.

I raise all my queries to chocolate and wine,
Where answers dissolve, sweet as pie, and divine.
Perhaps it's the giggles we stumble upon,
That carry our spirits until we are gone.

Dreams and Dilemmas

Can dreams really dance in the fields of our mind?
Or do they just giggle when we're stuck in a bind?
I ponder my breakfast, demand a retake,
While debating the reasons for toast with a flake.

Why do we worry about things that don't show?
Like socks on the road, or a friend's broken toe?
I smile at the worries that float in a stream,
As my cat ponders life while it chases a beam.

Would a donut debate with a slice of pie?
When the sprinkles are falling, they both start to fly.
I muse over moments that tick like a clock,
Yet all of my thoughts seem to giggle and mock.

In laughter and whim, I find bits of my day,
While scribbling nonsense, I drift and I sway.
Life, oh so puzzling, but wrapped up in cheer,
And maybe the meaning is simply right here.

Half-Truths and Full Lies

I asked the sage, what is the deal?
He said, my friend, it's all surreal.
With half the truth and laughs to share,
We're all just guessing, without a care.

I sought a map, but lost the thread,
Was it my fault or something said?
He chuckled softly, just let it be,
Life's a puzzle, not a decree.

With riddles wrapped in layers thick,
Deciphering life can feel quite slick.
But if we ponder, we might just find,
A twist or two can be quite kind.

So here we are, in this grand show,
Grinning wide with faces aglow.
Let's toast to chaos, embrace the jest,
In this big circus, we're all a guest.

The Map of Uncertainty

They say there's a map, but where is it found?
I checked my wallet; it's really unbound.
A dotted line to nowhere leads,
As I trip on dreams and fall through feeds.

To navigate life, I'm armed with a grin,
Yet mystery keeps pulling me in.
With signs that read 'Turn here!' and 'Go there!'
I twist and turn; it's all so rare.

The compass spins, it laughs at my plight,
It points to lunch instead of the light.
Maps filled with squiggles, no straight-ahead,
I'll take a detour; let's go to bread!

So here's to the paths that twist and play,
With lunch in hand, I'll find my way.
Navigating nonsense, that's my art,
In this grand maze, we all take part.

Shards of Clarity

In moments few, clarity strikes fast,
Like lightning glinting through a glass cast.
But just as quickly, it fades away,
Leaving me guessing the rest of the day.

A glimpse of sense, like a fleeting star,
Makes me ponder just how bizarre.
With cracks in wisdom spreading wide,
I laugh at the chaos, my cosmic guide.

I tried to catch it, the clear and bright,
But it slipped like sand into the night.
With shards around me, I trip on light,
And giggles bubble; the world feels right.

So here's to the laughter amid the doubt,
As life spills tricks, let's cheer and shout.
Embrace the mess, the fun, the flair,
In shards of clarity, we find our air.

Poems from the Edge

On the edge of reason, where nonsense calls,
I scribble thoughts as the laughter sprawls.
With whims and fancies, I dance on fate,
Turns out, life's just a quirky plate.

I peeked over life's precarious brink,
And saw the world winking, don't overthink!
A jester's smile hid wisdom so bright,
In every blunder, there's pure delight.

So let's tiptoe on these whims so grand,
As we play at life, hand in hand.
With rhymes of laughter, we'll chime and cheer,
Painting the edge with colors so clear.

Let's frolic in jest, not wear a frown,
For every hiccup is a gem in town.
In poems from the edge, we find glee,
Together, forever, just you and me.

Footprints in the Fog

Woke up this morning, coffee's my guide,
Thoughts drift like seagulls, where do they hide?
Life's a mystery, like socks in the wash,
Searching for answers, but feeling a squish.

Walking on pathways, footprints appear,
But the fog rolls in, and they disappear.
Chasing my thoughts, but they run away,
What is the lesson in this daily play?

Laughter is golden, or so they all say,
Yet here I am, lost in the fray.
Should I just dance, twirl with delight?
Or ponder forever through long, lonely nights?

So cheers to the puzzling, the fun of the chase,
I'll tip my hat to this curious race.
In foggy adventures where laughter can bloom,
Finding myself in the most silly room.

Scraps of Wisdom

Eating my breakfast, a toast with a grin,
Reading the news, where to even begin?
They say life's a journey, but here's my thought,
Shouldn't it come with a map and a plot?

I gathered some wisdom from memes on my phone,
Between cat videos and pizza on loan.
"Just live for the moment," the internet said,
Yet my moments vanish, I just want some bread!

Experts say love is the answer we seek,
But why do my socks always go missing each week?
Wisdom is funny, elusive like fog,
Maybe it's life that's the biggest old hog?

So let's raise a glass to the nonsense we find,
For laughter and chaos bring joy to our mind.
In scraps of confusion, a treasure may lie,
I'll just keep on smiling as the days drift by.

The Dilemma of Knowing

Waking up puzzled, what's on the agenda?
Life's a big puzzle, and I've lost the Menda.
Is knowledge a gift, or a curse in disguise?
The more I learn, the more I realize.

Questions like bubbles float through my mind,
Blowing them gently, but what do I find?
Should I seek answers, or just play along?
Maybe I'll start a new dance with a song.

Philosophers chat, with their frowns and their glasses,
Who knew that wisdom comes wrapped in molasses?
I'll skip the debates, and just go for a snack,
Life's too short to stay lost in that stack.

So here's to the puzzle, the wise and the silly,
Let's laugh at the questions, the quirks that thrill me.
In this grand dilemma of clever and fun,
I'll just be myself till the day is all done.

In the Shadow of Meaning

In the bright shadows of everyday fun,
I chase silly meanings, oh what have I spun?
Life always giggles when I take a peek,
Climbing up questions, then feeling so weak.

Dancing in circles, but where do I go?
The signs point to wisdom, but they tease me slow.
I ponder my thoughts, like ducks in a line,
Quacking about purpose, is it silly or fine?

Some wear deep frowns, calling life a tough race,
While I wear a grin, with cake on my face.
Meaning's elusive, like bubbles that pop,
But where's the fun in just stopping? Let's hop!

So let's build a castle of laughter and cheer,
Making up meanings that vanish like air.
In shadows of jest, where the giggles reside,
I'll celebrate life with my friends by my side.

www.ingramcontent.com/pod-product-compliance
Lightning Source LLC
Chambersburg PA
CBHW051654160426
43209CB00004B/889